THE BEST
IS YET
TO BE

Edited by
Susan Polis Schutz

Designed and illustrated by
Stephen Schutz

**Blue
Mountain
Arts**, inc.

Boulder, Colorado

Library of Congress Catalog: 74-81781
ISBN Number: 0-88396-005-2

Manufactured in the United States of America

First Printing: July, 1974
Second Printing: October, 1974
Third Printing: February, 1975
Fourth Printing: October, 1975

ACKNOWLEDGEMENTS are on page 63.

BLUE MOUNTAIN ARTS, INC.
P.O. Box 4549
Boulder, Colorado. 80302

CONTENTS

INTRODUCTION

Growing older, as shown by the philosophy expressed in *The Best is Yet to Be*, is a beautiful phenomenon. Unfortunately, in our society, people think old age is a time to retire from life. Our elders cannot get jobs and are forced to live on an impossibly low income. The problems of older people are ignored. There is an extreme overemphasis on youth. Talk like youth! Look like youth! Act like youth! This trend is anti-growing old, which essentially is anti-life. Legislation is needed to provide creative jobs and a better income for older people. But there will be no real change in our society until our attitudes change.

With age comes the wisdom and knowledge of experience. So, in fact, it is our elders who should be sought after for jobs. And it is our elders whom we should honor.

I hope that the poems in this book stimulate us to a more complete appreciation of life.

Susan Polis Schutz

Grow old along with me!
The best is yet to be,
The last of life, for which the first
   was made:
Our times are in his hand
Who saith "A whole I planned,
Youth shows but half; trust God:
   see all, nor be afraid!"

Robert Browning

Age is a quality of mind.
If you have left your dreams behind,
If hope is cold,
If you no longer look ahead,
If your ambitions' fires are dead—
Then you are old.
But if from life you take the best,
If in life you keep the jest,
If love you hold;
No matter how the years go by,
No matter how the birthdays fly—
You are not old.

H. S. Fritsch

"How Old
are you?"

The longer I live
the more my mind
dwells upon the
beauty and the wonder
of the world.

John Burroughs

Oh for one hour of youthful joy!
    Give back my twentieth spring!
I'd rather laugh, a bright-haired boy,
    Than reign, a gray-beard king.

Off with the spoils of wrinkled age!
    Away with Learning's crown!
Tear out life's Wisdom-written page,
    And dash its trophies down!

One moment let my life-blood stream
    From boyhood's fount of flame!
Give me one giddy, reeling dream
    Of life all love and fame!

My listening angel heard the prayer,
    And, calmly smiling, said,
"If I but touch thy silvered hair,
    Thy hasty wish hath sped.

"But is there nothing in thy track
    To bid thee fondly stay,
While the swift seasons hurry back
    To find the wished-for day?"

"Ah, truest soul of womankind!
    Without thee what were life?
One bliss I cannot leave behind:
    I'll take — my — precious — wife!"

The angel took a sapphire pen
    And wrote in rainbow dew,
The man would be a boy again,
    And be a husband, too!

"And is there nothing yet unsaid,
    Before the change appears?
Remember, all their gifts have fled
    With those dissolving years."

"Why, yes," for memory would recall
    My fond paternal joys;
"I could not bear to leave them all —
    I'll take — my — girl — and — boys."

The smiling angel dropped his pen, —
    "Why, this will never do;
The man would be a boy again,
    And be a father, too!"

And so I laughed, — my laughter woke
    The household with its noise, —
And wrote my dream, when morning broke,
    To please the gray-haired boys.

                    Oliver Wendell Holmes

The whole secret of remaining young
in spite of years, and even of gray hairs,
is to cherish enthusiasm in oneself, by
poetry, by contemplation, by charity, — that
is, in fewer words, by the maintenance
of harmony in the soul. When everything is
in its right place within us, we
ourselves are in equilibrium with the whole
work of God. Deep and grave enthusiasm
for the eternal beauty and the eternal order,
reason touched with emotion and a
serene tenderness of heart — these surely are
the foundations of wisdom.

Amiel

Gray hairs seem to my fancy like
the soft light of the moon, silvering
over the evening of life.

Richter

Let me grow lovely, growing old—
  So many fine things do;
Laces and ivory, and gold,
  And silks need not be new;

And there is healing in old trees,
  Old streets a glamour hold;
Why may not I, as well as these,
  Grow lovely, growing old?

Karle Wilson Baker

THE ROAD NOT TAKEN

Two roads diverged in a yellow wood,
And sorry I could not travel both
And be one traveler, long as I stood
And looked down one as far as I could
To where it bent in the undergrowth;

Then took the other, as just as fair,
And having perhaps the better claim,
Because it was grassy and wanted wear;
Though as for that, the passing there
Had worn them really about the same,

And both that morning equally lay
In leaves no step had trodden black.
Oh, I kept the first for another day!
Yet knowing how way leads on to way,
I doubted if I should ever come back.

I shall be telling this with a sigh
Somewhere ages and ages hence:
Two roads diverged in a wood, and I—
I took the one less traveled by,
And that has made all the difference.

Robert Frost

My heart leaps up when I behold
    A Rainbow in the sky:
So was it when my life began;
So is it now I am a Man;
So be it when I shall grow old,
    Or let me die!
The Child is Father of the Man;
And I could wish my days to be
Bound each to each by natural piety.

William Wordsworth

Loveliest of trees, the cherry now
Is hung with bloom along the bough,
And stands about the woodland ride
Wearing white for Eastertide.

Now, of my threescore years and ten,
Twenty will not come again,
And take from seventy springs a score,
It only leaves me fifty more.

And since to look at things in bloom
Fifty springs are little room,
About the woodlands I will go
To see the cherry hung with snow.

A. E. Housman

There are those
Whom time can never age — not even with years;
These keep a dream, not let its flame burn low . . .
They look ahead, beyond regrets and tears —
Old age is something they can never know.

"When the Gods Love"

Margaret E. Bruner

**To be seventy years young
is sometimes far more
cheerful and hopeful
than to be forty years old.**

Oliver Wendell Holmes

"The Old Man's Dream"

I work or play, as I think best;
　　I fare abroad, or stay at home;
When weary, I sit down and rest;
　　I bid one go, another come —
　　　Because I'm sixty!

When whistles blow with clamorous hue,
　　I rouse me not, as I was wont.
I do the things I like to do,
　　And leave undone the things I don't —
　　　Because I'm sixty!

I grow not blind, nor deaf, nor lame,
　　I still can dance, and hear, and see,
But love the restful book or game;
　　No more the strenuous life for me,
　　　I quit at sixty!

My toilet is my fondest care,
　　The serial story I peruse;
I glory in my silvering hair,
　　I love my comfortable shoes —
　　　I'm glad I'm sixty!

Let youngsters lift the weary load,
　　And at the burden tug and strain:
I love the easy, downward road;
　　I would not climb life's hill again —
　　　Glory be! I'm sixty!

Anonymous

Old age and the wear of time teach many things.

Sophocles

Let us cherish and love old age; for it is full of pleasure, if one knows how to use it. . . .

Seneca

Yes, I may walk a little slower
     and old they may call me
But I look a little longer
     at each dawn that breaks for me
I hear a little better
     all the sounds a day can hold
I love a whole lot stronger
     all the worldly births I see unfold

I see a little clearer
     what the world holds out to me
I feel a whole lot deeper
     for another's misery
I dream a lot more often
     of the days that long have past
I acknowledge precious time
     that ticks away so fast

I hold a great deal tighter
     to loving friends' embraces
And oh, how I cherish laughing children
     with life's smudges on their faces
Yes, I may walk a little slower
     and old they may call me
But do you know, I see, I hear and I love
     much better than that young girl
        I used to be.

Bobbie Soutar

If you haven't a few face lines then you haven't
really lived. Palm lines reveal what can be.
Face lines reveal what was. They begin like little
seedlings. Sunny days and rainy days make
them grow. Take for instance my face lines.

The one above, up near my brow, came from
twenty years of, "Why not mom", "Ah gee",
"Why can't I go out" and "How mom how".
The little skinny ones, faint but there,
began to grow when my number one son
began to ignore the barber's chair.
This crooked one etched deep and hard,
seems to thrive on school report cards.
My huge bumpy one that connects
my eyes with one big lump
came from four rounds of measles,
chicken pox, strep throat and mumps.
The gay one that swirls in circles alike,
started to travel when Jr. started
to travel on his gold and white bike.
The others are happiness lines that you see,
when I think how lucky I am
that this family belongs to me.

So, don't waste your precious gift of laughter
and immunize yourself from strife.
Only a face made of plaster
is immobilized to life.
Oh no, face lines are a treasure.
Be proud when yours begin to show.
My goodness, what on earth good
is a lovely cover if
the inside could not show.

Bobbie Soutar

A fruitful mind
combined with a compassionate heart
keeps you alive and young.

David Polis

Your feet may not run as fast as your mind
but remember that there are a number of people
much younger whose minds cannot keep up
with their feet.

David Polis

Make new friends, but keep the old;
Those are silver, these are gold.
New-made friendships, like new wine,
Age will mellow and refine.
Friendships that have stood the test —
Time and change — are surely best;
Brow may wrinkle, hair grow gray,
Friendship never knows decay.
For 'mid old friends, tried and true,
Once more we our youth renew.
But old friends, alas! may die,
New friends must their place supply.
Cherish friendship in your breast —
New is good, but old is best;
Make new friends, but keep the old;
Those are silver, these are gold.

Joseph Parry

Strange—to grow up and not be different,
Not beautiful or even very wise . . .
No winging-out the way of butterflies,
No sudden blindfold-lifting from the eyes.

Strange—to grow up and still be wondering,
Reverent at petals and snow,
Still holding breath,
Still often tiptoe,
Questioning dew and stars,
Wanting to know!

Mildred Bowers Armstrong

Half the job of life is in
little things taken on the run.
Let us run if we must —
even the sands do that —
but let us keep our hearts young
and our eyes open that nothing
worth our while shall escape us.
And everything is worth its while
if we only grasp it
and its significance.

Victor Cherbuliez

Measured by the achievements
of the years I have seen, I am one of the oldest
men who have ever lived; but I do not
feel old, and I propose to give you the recipe
by which I have preserved my youth.
I have always given a friendly welcome to new
ideas, and I have endeavored not to feel
too old to learn, and thus, though I stand here
with the snows of so many winters upon
my head, my faith in human nature, my belief
in the progress of man to a better social
condition, and especially my trust in the ability
of men to establish and maintain self-
government, are as fresh and as young as
when I began to travel the path of life.

Peter Cooper

Lucky is he who
can get his grapes to market
and keep the bloom upon them,
who can carry some of the freshness
and eagerness and simplicity
of youth into his later years,
who can have a boy's heart
below a man's head.

John Burroughs

Ere I am old—that time is now;
For youth sits lightly on my brow:
My limbs are firm, and strong, and free;
Life hath a thousand charms for me—
Charms that will long their influence hold
Within my heart—ere I am old.

Ere I am old, O! let me give
My life to learning how to live . . . .

Caroline Atherton Briggs Mason

Youth was the time for searching
Trying to find one's self.
Attempting to know one's self.
Roaming in many directions to
        find the answers.

With maturity the search ended.
The peace and quiet of standing still.
The friendship with one's self.
The acceptance of one's faults.
The knowledge of one's strengths.
And, thankfully and happily, the feeling
        each morning of liking one's self.

June Polis

Youth is not a time of life—it is a state of mind.
It is not a matter of red cheeks, red lips and supple
knees. It is a temper of the will; a quality
of the imagination; a vigor of the emotions; it is a
freshness of the deep springs of life. Youth means
a temperamental predominance of courage
over timidity, of the appetite for adventure over a
life of ease. This often exists in a man of fifty,
more than in a boy of twenty. Nobody grows old by
merely living a number of years; people grow
old by deserting their ideals.

Years may wrinkle the skin, but to give up
enthusiasm wrinkles the soul. Worry, doubt, self-
distrust, fear and despair—these are the long,
long years that bow the head and turn the growing
spirit back to dust.

Whether seventy or sixteen, there is in every
being's heart a love of wonder; the sweet
amazement at the stars and starlike things and
thoughts; the undaunted challenge of events,
the unfailing, childlike appetite for what comes
next, and the joy in the game of life.

You are as young as your faith, as old as your doubt; as young as your self-confidence, as old as your fear; as young as your hope, as old as your despair.

In the central place of your heart there is a wireless station. So long as it receives messages of beauty, hope, cheer, grandeur, courage and power from the earth, from men and from the Infinite — so long are you young. When the wires are all down and the central places of your heart are covered with the snows of pessimism and the ice of cynicism, then you are grown old, indeed!

Samuel Ullman

I know, as my life grows older,
    And mine eyes have clearer sight,
That under each rank wrong somewhere
    There lies the root of Right;

That each sorrow has its purpose,
    By the sorrowing oft unguessed;
But as sure as the sun brings morning,
    Whatever is — is best.

I know that each sinful action,
    As sure as the night brings shade,
Is somewhere, sometime punished,
    Tho' the hour be long delayed.
I know that the soul is aided
    Sometimes by the heart's unrest,
And to grow means often to suffer —
    But whatever is — is best.

I know there are no errors,
    In the great Eternal plan,
And all things work together
    For the final good of man.
And I know when my soul speeds onward,
    In its grand Eternal quest,
I shall say as I look back earthward,
    Whatever is — is best.

Ella Wheeler Wilcox

It is in old men that reason and judgment are found, and had it not been for old men no state would have existed at all.

Cicero

It is too late! Ah, nothing is too late
Till the tired heart shall cease to palpitate.
Cato learned Greek at eighty; Sophocles
Wrote his grand Oedipus, and Simonides
Bore off the prize of verse from his compeers,

When each had numbered more than fourscore years,
And Theophrastus, at fourscore and ten,
Had but begun his "Characters of Men."
Chaucer, at Woodstock with the nightingales,
At sixty wrote the Canterbury Tales;
Goethe at Weimar, toiling to the last,
Completed Faust when eighty years were past.

Henry Wadsworth Longfellow

When we were young and filled with elation
We gave no thought to future anticipation.
The carefree years passed all too soon.
And, men were walking on the moon.

Our goals in life were many.
In progress we believed.
We struggled in life's maelstrom.
Success we have achieved.
The tension of our younger years
Has definitely eased.
A new horizon brightens —
We can do just as we please.

Louise C. Odin

Remember the days of summer
 the days wrapped in the rays of gold
Once in awhile think of the butterflies
  decorating the sky like ornaments
      off a Christmas tree
Remember these and you can never grow old
  For you have witnessed Nature's soul
Forever beautiful
   Forever free . . . . .

Linger upon the memories of autumn
 memories burnished with each turning leaf
Ponder the miracle which brings the geese south
  landing on our lakes with one graceful sweep
Remember these and you can never grow old
  For you have witnessed Nature's soul
Forever wild
   May it always be . . . . .

And then those chill days of winter
   days cold, stark and bare
Reminisce of times warmed by the fire's soft glow
    casting and molding our dreams with each
                  spark and dancing flame
Remember these and you can never grow old
    For you have witnessed Nature's soul
Forever unique
       May it seem . . . . .

Relive each day of spring
   green, new days alive with explosive buds
Cherish the newness found in the waters, woods,
   fields and sky, portraits composed of
   the first fireflies and April shower's first
                  mud puddle
Remember these and you can never grow old
    For you have witnessed Nature's soul
Forever
     Let it be.

Susan Smith

Youth is like a
fresh flower in May.
Age is like a rainbow
that follows the storms of life.
Each has its own beauty.

David Polis

We have lived and loved together
  Through many changing years;
We have shared each other's gladness
  And wept each other's tears;
I have known ne'er a sorrow
  That was long unsoothed by thee;
For thy smiles can make a summer
  Where darkness else would be.

Like the leaves that fall around us
  In autumn's fading hours,
Are the traitor's smiles, that darken
  When the cloud of sorrow lowers;
And though many such we've known, love,
  Too prone, alas, to range,
We both can speak of one love
  Which time can never change.

We have lived and loved together
  Through many changing years,
We have shared each other's gladness
  And wept each other's tears.
And let us hope the future,
  As the past has been will be:
I will share with thee my sorrows,
  And thou thy joys with me.

Charles Jefferys

Old age, to the unlearned, is winter;
to the learned, it is harvest time.

Yiddish Proverb

ACKNOWLEDGEMENTS

We gratefully acknowledge the permissions granted by the following authors, publishers, and authors' representatives to reprint poems from their publications. Recognition is also made to poets and original publishers for the use of many poems which are now in the public domain.

Holt, Rinehart and Winston, Inc. for "Loveliest of Trees, The Cherry Now", from "A Shropshire Lad" — Authorized Edition — from THE COLLECTED POEMS of A. E. HOUSMAN. Copyright 1939, 1940, © 1965 by Holt, Rinehart and Winston, Inc. Copyright © 1967, 1968 by Robert E. Symons. Reprinted by permission of Holt, Rinehart and Winston, Inc. Also to The Literary Trustees of Walter de la Mare, and the Society of Authors, as their representatives, for "Loveliest of Trees, The Cherry Now".

Hazel Felleman Powell for "New Friends and Old Friends" by Joseph Parry, "We Have Lived And Loved Together" by Charles Jefferys, "Whatever Is — Is Best" by Ella Wheeler Wilcox and "When I Am Old" by Caroline Atherton Briggs Mason from THE BEST LOVED POEMS OF THE AMERICAN PEOPLE published by Doubleday.

Hazel Felleman Powell for "Youth" by Samuel Ullman, "How Old Are You" by H. S. Fritsch, "Whom The Gods Love" by Margaret E. Bruner and "The Old Man's Dream" by Oliver Wendell Holmes from POEMS THAT LIVE FOREVER published by Doubleday.

Yale University Press for "Strange" by Mildred Bowers Armstrong. Copyright © 1928 by Yale University Press.

From the POETRY OF ROBERT FROST, "The Road Not Taken" by Robert Frost. Edited by Edward Connery Lathem. Copyright 1916, © 1969 by Holt, Rinehart and Winston, Inc. Copyright 1944 by Robert Frost. Reprinted by permission of Holt, Rinehart and Winston, Inc.

We would like to thank the following people for granting us permission to publish their poems for the first time. Bobbie Soutar for "Face Lines", and "I May Walk A Little Slower". Louise C. Odin for "The Elective Years". Susan K. Smith for "Nature's Soul". David Polis for "A Fruitful Mind", "Your Feet May Not Run", and "Youth is Like" and June Polis for "Youth Was The Time".

A careful effort has been made to trace the ownership of poems used in this anthology in order to get permission to reprint copyright poems and to give proper credit to the copyright owners.

If any error or omission has occurred, it is completely inadvertent, and we would like to correct it in future editions provided that written notification is made to the publisher, BLUE MOUNTAIN ARTS, INC., P.O. Box 4549, Boulder Colorado 80302.

Frostiana — Robert Frost